5th Edition

Ambulatory Care Nursing
Review Questions

American Academy of Ambulatory Care Nursing
Many settings. Multiple roles. One unifying specialty.

Ambulatory Care Nursing Review Questions
Fifth Edition

Stephanie G. Witwer, PhD, RN, NEA-BC, FAAN
Editor

Copyright © 2020
American Academy of Ambulatory Care Nursing (AAACN)
East Holly Avenue, Box 56, Pitman, NJ 08071-0056
800-AMB-NURS; FAX 856-589-7463; Email: aaacn@aaacn.org; www.aaacn.org

FIFTH EDITION
ISBN: 978-1-940325-63-7

All rights reserved. No part of this publication may be reproduced or transmitted in any form or by any means, electronic or mechanical, including photocopying, recording, or any information storage and retrieval system, without the written permission of the American Academy of Ambulatory Care Nursing.

Printed in the United States of America

Publication Management
Anthony J. Jannetti, Inc.
East Holly Avenue, Box 56, Pitman, NJ 08071-0056
856-256-2300; FAX 856-589-7463; www.ajj.com

Suggested Citation
American Academy of Ambulatory Care Nursing. (2020). *Ambulatory care nursing review questions* (5th Ed). S. Witwer (Ed.). Pitman, NJ: Author.

Notice: Care has been taken to confirm the accuracy of information presented and to ensure that treatments, practices, and procedures are accurate and conform to standards accepted at the time of publication. Constant changes in information resulting from continuing research and clinical experience, reasonable differences in opinions among authorities, unique aspects of individual clinical situations, and the possibility of human error in preparing such a publication require that the reader exercise individual judgment when making a clinical decision and, if necessary, consult and compare information from other authorities, professionals, and/or sources. Any procedure or practice described in this book should be applied by the health care practitioner under appropriate supervision in accordance with professional standards of care used with regard to the unique circumstances that apply in each practice situation.

Every effort has been made to ensure drug selections and dosages are in accordance with current recommendations and practice. Because of ongoing research, changes in government regulations, and the constant flow of information on drug therapy, reactions, and interactions, the reader is cautioned to check the package insert for each drug for indications, dosages, warnings, and precautions, particularly if the drug is new or infrequently used.

The authors, reviewers, editors, and publishers cannot accept any responsibility for errors or omissions or for any consequences from application of the information in this book and make no warranty, expressed or implied, with respect to the contents of the book.

Disclaimer: These review questions provide an opportunity to assess your knowledge of selected components of ambulatory care nursing practice and to practice answering multiple-choice items. They do not represent a comprehensive compilation of all content composing ambulatory care nursing practice. Completion of these test questions does not guarantee the examinee will pass the certification exam.

The editor, authors, and reviewers of these study questions are NOT item writers or content expert panel members for the Ambulatory Care Nursing Certification Examination offered by the American Nurses Credentialing Center.

The names used in the case examples in this publication are fictitious and are in no way based on any real or actual patient or health care provider.

Editor
Stephanie G. Witwer, PhD, RN, NEA-BC, FAAN

AAACN Members Contributing to the 5th Edition Questions

Cynthia Cadiente, MSN-NED
Dianne Cirillo, MS, RN-BC
Pamella Guntrum, DNP, MSN, RN-BC, AHN-BC
Cara Hough, BSN, RN-BC
Carlissa Kelly, MSN, RN-BC

Robin Pleshaw, MSN, RN-BC
Yessenia N. Sinclair, Major USAF, NC, RN-BC, MHA, MBA
Mary E. Sizer, DNP, RN, CPN
Danielle Smith, MSN, RN, CNL
Stephanie Witwer, PhD, RN, NEA-BC, FAAN

Reviewers

Michele Boyd, MSN, RN
Denise Hannagan, MSN, MHA, RN-BC, EDAC
Cynthia Nowicki Hnatiuk, EdD, RN, CAE
E. Mary Johnson, BSN, RN-C, NE-BC

Candia Baker Laughlin, MS, RN
Nancy May, DNP, RN-BC, NEA-BC
Susan Paschke, MSN, RN-BC, NEA-BC

Introduction

Welcome to the *Ambulatory Care Nursing Review Questions, 5th edition*, published by the American Academy of Ambulatory Care Nursing (AAACN). This set of practice test items is designed to assist ambulatory care nurses in assessing their knowledge of the practice of ambulatory care nursing. Professional nurses should take every opportunity to advance their expertise, skills, and knowledge, and use tools such as this publication to assess their knowledge gaps and learn from studying the answers.

All review questions, answers, and their associated page numbers (found in the back of the booklet) are based on the *Core Curriculum for Ambulatory Care Nursing, 4th edition* (Laughlin & Witwer, 2019), a AAACN publication. Using the *Core Curriculum* as the companion to this set of review questions is highly recommended.

This edition of the *Review Questions* has been updated to reflect the latest test content outline of the Ambulatory Care Nursing Certification Exam of the American Nurses Credentialing Center (ANCC) published in 2017. The 180 multiple-choice items follow the same format as the questions on the ANCC Ambulatory Care Nursing Certification Exam. The multiple-choice items are grouped into five domains of practice corresponding to those on the examination. The content in each of the domains and the percentage of questions are drawn directly from the test content outline as published by ANCC at the time of this writing (see Table 1).

Table 1.
Domains of Practice, ANCC Ambulatory Care Nursing Certification Test Content Outline, 2017

Category	Domains of Practice	Number of Questions	Percent
I	Clinical Practice	76	50.67%
II	Communication	34	22.67%
III	Professional Role	9	6.00%
IV	Systems/Legal and Regulatory	16	10.67%
V	Education	15	10.00%
Total		150	100.00%

Exam Information

For further information about the Ambulatory Care Nursing Certification Exam offered by ANCC, contact ANCC at 800-284-2378 or visit the ANCC website at https://www.nursingworld.org.

The exam is computer-based, containing 175 questions, 150 of which are scored and 25 are pilot questions. The test-taker does not know which questions are scored and which are not. Complete application and testing information may be found online at the ANCC website. Nurses can apply throughout the year and take the test any time within a 90-day window after the application is approved by ANCC. The test may be taken at Prometric testing centers (www.prometric.com/ancc).

Further information about the test content, some sample questions, and references used by the test item writers may also be found at the ANCC website https://www.nursingworld.org.

The American Academy of Ambulatory Care Nursing offers an array of exam preparation resources:
- *Ambulatory Care Nursing Orientation and Competency Assessment Guide, 3rd edition*
- *Core Curriculum for Ambulatory Care Nursing, 4th edition*
- *Scope and Standards of Practice for Professional Ambulatory Care Nursing, 9th edition*
- *Scope and Standards of Practice for Professional Telehealth Nursing, 6th edition*

Additionally, AAACN offers other exam preparation resources including the *Ambulatory Care Nursing Certification Review Course.* The all-day review course is taught live at the AAACN Annual Conference. The course is also available in the AAACN Online Library (https://library.aaacn.org/aaacn), and through a group access program for multiple groups of nurses. The course can also be presented at your location – call the AAACN National Office for details. An *Ambulatory Care Nursing Certification Review Course Syllabus* is also available.

Recommendations for Using These Review Questions

1. Complete all multiple-choice items or focus upon the items specific to one or more of the categories (see Table 1).
2. Read each multiple-choice item carefully and circle your answer on the Answer Sheets provided at the end of this publication.
    - Try to answer the question before reading options.
    - Underline key words.
    - Do not read anything more into the question or options than what is there; do not over analyze.
    - If unsure of the answer, use logic to rule out options that could be correct versus those that are definitely incorrect.
    - Select options that reflect a nursing judgment.
    - If two answers are correct, choose the one that causes the other to occur.
    - Select options that are correct without exception.
    - When evaluating difficult test questions, mark out the options you think are wrong.
    - Avoid options that are true statements, but do not answer the question.
3. Check for the correct answers using the Answer Key located at the end of this publication. For further information about the topic addressed in the question and the rationale for the answer given, reference the *Core Curriculum for Ambulatory Care, 4th edition*, and the page listed.
4. There is no passing score for this assessment. Reward yourself for the items you answer correctly. Review those items that you answer incorrectly to determine your areas for further study.

Reference

Laughlin, C.B., & Witwer, S.G. (Eds.). (2019). *Core curriculum for ambulatory care nursing* (4th ed.). American Academy of Ambulatory Care Nursing.

Clinical Practice

Questions 1-90

Questions 1 through 4 pertain to the same scenario.

1. Christopher, a 5-year-old with mild persistent asthma, presents in clinic with an acute upper-respiratory infection. He is accompanied by his mother. Which of the following is true about asthma?
   A. Air exchange into the blood stream in the alveoli is impaired by mucus.
   B. Chronically inflamed airways are hyper-responsive to triggers.
   C. Pulse oximetry is the best method for assessing asthma control at home.
   D. Symptoms include continual wheezing, coughing, and chest discomfort.

2. Christopher's mother reports his symptoms had been significantly better for the past month, so she has not refilled his costly medications for several weeks. Which of the medications was most likely to have been prescribed daily for control of Christopher's mild persistent asthma?
   A. Oral corticosteroid
   B. Oral bronchodilator
   C. Low-dose inhaled corticosteroid
   D. Inhaled short-acting beta-2 antagonist

3. Christopher's peak flow rate today is 70% of his personal best rate. What does this indicate?
   A. Green zone – good control of asthma. Continue with current medication plan.
   B. Blue zone – moderate control of asthma. Continue long-acting drug and monitor closely.
   C. Yellow zone – caution. Take quick relief medication and monitor.
   D. Red zone – danger. Take quick relief drug and seek medical care if no immediate response.

4. Christopher's mother has some misperceptions about asthma. Which one of the following beliefs about asthma is true?
   A. Asthma is linked to select mental health diagnoses.
   B. Asthma medications can lose effectiveness over time, so they should be used sparingly.
   C. Even if his asthma is controlled, Christopher should limit his physical activity and avoid strenuous exercise.
   D. Asthma exacerbations rarely occur suddenly, without any warning signs.

5. An adult patient calls the clinic for advice about self-care for symptoms of sinusitis. The nursing intervention should include:
   A. Advising increased fluids and humidification.
   B. Determining the color and amount of nasal drainage.
   C. Assessing facial pain using a 10-point scale.
   D. Determining the effectiveness of over-the-counter (OTC) decongestants.

6. Vincent, age 46, has recently been diagnosed with pulmonary tuberculosis. He stated that he has been feeling ill for several weeks, but sought medical attention when he began coughing up bloody secretions. Which of the following symptoms are also experienced commonly by persons with active tuberculosis?
   A. Increased appetite and weight gain
   B. Fatigue, lymph node enlargement, and night sweats
   C. Slow pulse rate, edema, and warm, dry skin
   D. High fever and shaking chills

7. The mother of a 3-year-old boy, Chase, calls the primary care clinic for advice about Chase's fever. She reports Chase does not appear to be uncomfortable, is playing quietly, and is eating and drinking, but his temperature is 101.0° F orally. The nurse should recommend which of the following?
   A. Administer acetaminophen, dosing according to the guidelines on the clinic website.
   B. Administer acetaminophen if temperature exceeds 102° F orally, and alternate with ibuprofen according to clinic guidelines.
   C. Dress in lightweight clothing and avoid overdressing. Avoid bundling blankets.
   D. Sponge with lukewarm water to lower Chase's temperature but avoid chilling him.

8. Which of the following is an example of primary prevention?
   A. Sex education
   B. Biopsy of a skin lesion
   C. Mammogram
   D. Use of lipid-lowering drugs

Clinical Practice

Questions 1-90

9. Telephone triage is:
   A. All care and services provided within the scope of nursing practice that are delivered via the telephone.
   B. An interaction that occurs over the telephone involving identification of the nature and urgency of the client's health care needs and determination of the appropriate disposition.
   C. The delivery of health services that integrate electronic information and telecommunications technology to promote access in an efficient and high-quality manner.
   D. The delivery, management, and coordination of health care services provided via telecommunication technology.

10. Which of the following examples would **best** describe a nurse appropriately using clinical reasoning in telephone nursing?
    A. A nurse who tells a child's mother that based on cough intensity, the child may have pneumonia.
    B. A nurse advises a patient that their chest pain might just be indigestion and not to worry.
    C. A nurse asking how many episodes of diarrhea the oncology patient had today while on chemotherapy.
    D. A nurse recognizing that sudden facial numbness and slurred speech are signs of a stroke.

11. A 26-year-old female patient calls the clinic and states that she has the "worst pain I've ever had" in her abdomen. The nurse should:
    A. Refer her immediately to an emergency department.
    B. Instruct her to call 9-1-1.
    C. Ask to speak to another member of the household to verify the intensity of the pain.
    D. Further assess the characteristics and location of the pain and related symptoms.

12. A nurse practices in an organization that uses online protocols to guide telehealth nursing practice. The value of a set of decision support tools is that the tools:
    A. Replace having to apply the nursing process to meet patient needs, so may be used by assistive personnel.
    B. Serve as a checklist to increase the likelihood that nothing of importance is overlooked.
    C. Improve the probability that the care recommended will be covered and reimbursed by third-party payers.
    D. Are more reliable than hard copy books of protocols.

13. A 53-year-old woman calls complaining of acute low-back pain after a long day of gardening. The pain increases with movement, so she has been resting on her family room couch, trying to stay as still as possible. The nurse has ruled out underlying disease processes per protocol and has concluded the pain is most likely due to muscle strain. In developing a self-care plan with the patient, which of the following would be nurse's **best** recommendation?
    A. Continue to rest on the couch for a day or two, taking nonsteroidal anti-inflammatory drugs (NSAIDS) every 4-6 hours.
    B. The couch is probably too soft. Instead, rest on a firm surface for a day or two, with knees bent instead. Take NSAIDs.
    C. Maintain activities as tolerated. Bed rest is not recommended.
    D. Heat compresses to the back when resting is recommended.

14. In school-aged children with acute vomiting, rehydration therapy would **best** include which of the following?
    A. Half-strength sports drinks
    B. Half-strength fruit juices
    C. Flat soft drink
    D. Protein drinks

15. A nurse finds an unconscious elderly woman on the floor in the clinic restroom. After establishing unresponsiveness, the nurse's **first** action is to:
    A. Check for breathing and call for help.
    B. Move patient to an area where the clinicians can better treat her and activate Emergency Medical Services (EMS).
    C. Begin chest compressions and rescue breathing in a 30:2 ratio.
    D. Obtain the automatic external defibrillator and apply pads to assess the need for defibrillation.

16. John, age 25, is brought to the front desk of the outpatient clinic by his very anxious friends. They say John complained suddenly of lightheadedness and shortness of breath while they were playing basketball outdoors. They think he may have been stung by an insect. The nurse should first:
    A. Prepare to administer epinephrine 1:1,000 dilution, 0.3-0.5 ml.
    B. Assess for increased blood pressure.
    C. Try to get John to relax and do pursed-lip breathing.
    D. Assess airway and vital signs; notify EMS.

Clinical Practice Questions 1-90

17. A 2-year-old's father has called to report the child is crying inconsolably and pulling on his left ear. He says the child has had ear infections before, and he has amoxicillin left over from the last infection. He asks the triage nurse if he should start the child on amoxicillin while the nurse checks with the provider about an additional course of treatment. The nurse's **best** response would be:
    A. "Your child really needs to be evaluated by a physician or NP in our office to determine if this is an ear infection and how to best treat it."
    B. "No, because ear infections often resolve on their own without antibiotics. We recommend that you give him acetaminophen and decongestants and let us know if he doesn't get better."
    C. "No, because the amoxicillin may not be any good anymore."
    D. "The reason your child probably has repeated ear infections is that we no longer prescribe amoxicillin for ear infections. There is a different antibiotic which is now preferred."

18. Which of the following are signs of volume overload in a patient with chronic heart failure?
    A. Edema, neck vein distension, sudden weight gain
    B. Hypertension, fatigue, productive cough
    C. Night sweats, excess urination, cardiac arrhythmias
    D. Headache, weight loss, depression

19. A 26-year-old single parent of two young children, with very little income, asks the nurse about possible sources of help with health care expenses. Which government resources would the patient most likely to be eligible to receive?
    A. Medicare Parts A and B
    B. Medicare Part D
    C. TriCare
    D. Medicaid

20. In managing pain in culturally diverse populations, the following steps would be helpful for the nurse to develop cultural competency and humility **except for:**
    A. Delivering holistic care to patients as long as they are open and accepting of pain management plan.
    B. Re-envisioning how being human links people of various cultures together.
    C. Understanding one's own personal preconceived notions about different cultures.
    D. Developing relationships and acknowledging patients and caregivers in a professional and personal level.

21. In a family practice clinic, the nurse observes a medical assistant preparing to take the blood pressure (BP) of a 66-year-old for a general medical examination. Which of the following is **not** true?
    A. In addition to sitting, standing BP is recommended.
    B. The medical assistant should take the BP while the patient is seated on the exam table after waiting 5 minutes.
    C. Patients should abstain from smoking or drinking caffeinated beverages prior to the readings.
    D. The medical assistant should use a cuff with a bladder that covers two-thirds of the length of the upper arm and 80% of the circumference of the upper arm.

22. Which of the following is true about chronic obstructive pulmonary disease (COPD)?
    A. Airway limitation is fully reversible with medical therapies.
    B. Spirometry is required to establish the diagnosis of COPD.
    C. Cough is a symptom found only in later stages of the disease.
    D. Conjugated pneumococcal vaccine 13-valent (PCV-13) is routinely used to reduce the risk of community-acquired pneumococcal pneumonia in patients with COPD.

23. Which agency collects reports of medication-related hazards and disseminates medication safety information, risk-reduction tools, and error-prevention strategies?
    A. Institute for Safe Medication Practices
    B. Occupational Safety and Health Administration (OSHA)
    C. Centers for Disease Control and Prevention (CDC)
    D. United States Preventive Services Task Force (USPSTF)

24. Joshua is a 5-year-old with sickle cell disease. His mother called to report Joshua has a fever over 101.5° orally and mild leg pain. The nurse should:
    A. Advise the mother about the dose of acetaminophen or ibuprofen to administer orally and to call back if the fever does not go down.
    B. Tell the mother to bring Joshua in right away to be evaluated.
    C. Do a thorough pain assessment, including location, onset, and severity using an appropriate pain scale.
    D. Assess Joshua's fluid intake and output in the past several hours.

Clinical Practice

Questions 1-90

25. The statement that **best** describes prediabetes is:
    A. Prediabetes is irreversible and will develop into diabetes over time.
    B. The disease is a result of damaged pancreatic beta cells.
    C. Slightly elevated fasting blood glucose and hemoglobin A1C levels is typical with prediabetes.
    D. Oral diabetes medications are necessary to treat prediabetes.

26. Which of the following is the highest priority in the educational plan for a woman newly diagnosed with type 2 diabetes?
    A. Weigh daily and report variations in weight of 4 or more pounds per week.
    B. Psychological support to enhance coping skills.
    C. Recognize acute complications such as hyperglycemia or hypoglycemia, and when to seek medical advice.
    D. Carefully control diabetes to prevent complications including cardiovascular disease, loss of vision, neuropathy, and kidney damage.

Questions 27 and 28 pertain to the same scenario.

27. Joe is a 68-year-old patient with a 7-year history of type 2 diabetes. He also has a history of hypertension and hyperlipidemia. Recently his blood glucose control has become less stable, with episodes of hyperglycemia that cause polyuria, especially at night. Which of the following referral resources could help improve Joe's diabetes control?
    A. Endocrinologist, dietitian, mental health professional
    B. Endocrinologist, dietitian, clinical pharmacist
    C. Physical therapist, diabetes educator, home care nurse
    D. Social worker, physical therapist, neurologist

28. For Joe's hyperlipidemia, he has been prescribed simvastatin (Zocor®) 10 mg at bedtime daily. His lipid profile drawn yesterday shows his low-density lipoprotein cholesterol (LDL) is 180 mg/dl and his high-density lipoprotein cholesterol (HDL) is 25 mg/dl. What conclusion would you draw?
    A. His lipids are well controlled. No change is indicated.
    B. His lipids are not fully controlled and he may need to increase his simvastatin dosage.
    C. His lipids are not well controlled and a calcium channel blocker might be effective in further improving lipid levels.
    D. Since his lipids are only mildly out of range, lifestyle changes of limiting alcohol and sodium reduction would be sufficient to further improve the lipid control.

29. The following are elements of Dietary Approaches to Stop Hypertension (DASH):
    A. High protein, low carbohydrate, low sodium.
    B. Low-saturated fats, limited fruits and vegetables, low calcium.
    C. Low cholesterol and total fat, low fat dairy products, increased fruits and vegetables.
    D. Reduced red meats, low-fat dairy products, eight or more glasses of water per day.

30. Which of the following statements is true about palliative care?
    A. To be eligible, the patient must have a life expectancy of 6 months or less.
    B. Goals are to prevent and relieve suffering and support quality of life.
    C. It cannot be provided concurrently with life-prolonging treatment.
    D. During a hospitalization, palliative care will be discontinued.

31. James, age 65, has late-stage lung cancer. Although he is currently receiving chemotherapy, his health care team is preparing to talk to James and his wife about end-of-life care options. What should they anticipate in preparing for the discussion?
    A. James and his wife are aware of hospice and palliative care options.
    B. James may be worried that he will become a burden on his wife and family to provide all his care.
    C. Because James has Medicare, he will be aware of the hospice benefit coverage.
    D. James and his wife are confident his care needs will be better met through hospice or palliative care.

32. A patient is brought into the clinic by family members and collapses into a chair in the lobby. The family indicates it is possible the patient may have taken an unknown number of prescription opioids. Acute symptoms of opioid overdose include:
    A. Enlarged pupils, hyper-irritability.
    B. Small pupils, slurred speech, easily aroused.
    C. Petit mal seizures.
    D. Small pupils, unable to arouse, slow or stopped breathing.

Clinical Practice

Questions 1-90

33. Which of the following statements is true about depression in a patient with a terminal illness?
    A. Previous history of depression is unrelated to depression experienced with terminal illness.
    B. Patients experiencing depression with terminal illness often gain weight due to inactivity.
    C. Treatment of depression should focus on non-pharmacologic interventions because of the dangers of antidepressant medications in patients with failing body systems.
    D. Antidepressant medications may be helpful to improve pain control.

34. In preparing the family for a patient's imminent death, which of the following should be included in education?
    A. The signs and symptoms of dying that will occur first are weakness, fatigue, and decreased oral intake.
    B. The family may fear giving a dose of pain medication may hasten death.
    C. The dying process is a natural slowing down of body processes that occurs over 2 days.
    D. Increased energy or restlessness may signal an improvement in the body's response to illness.

35. Untreated hypertension may lead to target organ damage in which of the following?
    A. Eyes
    B. Lungs
    C. Liver
    D. Peripheral nerves

36. During nursing assessment, patients with chronic systolic heart failure should be questioned about the use of which of the following medications that can lead to decompensation?
    A. Calcium channel blockers, alpha blockers, and beta-adrenergic blockers
    B. Digoxin, amiodarone, and allopurinol
    C. Aspirin, warfarin, and antihistamines
    D. Decongestants, antacids, and nonsteroidal anti-inflammatory agents

37. Which of the following statements describes a person who is moderately sedated?
    A. May require assistance to maintain patent airway.
    B. Has temporary interruption of nerve impulse transmission to a specific area of the body.
    C. Has temporarily lost protective reflexes.
    D. Responds purposefully to verbal commands.

38. Which of the following is true about preoperative informed consent?
    A. A registered nurse (RN) should obtain consent, assuring that the patient understands the risks and benefits of the procedure, alternatives, and consequences of foregoing the procedure.
    B. If the patient is mentally incompetent, he or she cannot legally consent to the procedure.
    C. Staff members who sign as witnesses are attesting the patient is competent and understands the content of the consent form.
    D. Consent is needed for procedures having general anesthesia, but not necessary for moderate or deep-sedation procedures.

39. Mr. Buck is a 34-year-old patient who had repair of the meniscus in his left knee in the ambulatory surgery center. The procedure was arthroscopic and the patient was placed in a knee immobilizer. To discharge Mr. Buck to his home, which of the following conditions must be met?
    A. He needs to be able to crutch walk at least 100 yards.
    B. His temperature needs to be less than or equal to 99° F.
    C. He needs to have full sensation and movement of his left leg.
    D. He must have a ride home with a responsible adult.

40. A 50-year-old patient is instructed to collect three stool guaiac cards and mail them to the clinic for testing for microscopic blood. Which of the following should be part of the patient's instructions for the test?
    A. The guaiac test is routinely used for cancer screening.
    B. Do not collect a specimen if having loose stool or diarrhea.
    C. Avoid orange juice and high doses of vitamin C.
    D. Avoid taking aspirin and NSAIDS as they can lead to a false negative result.

Clinical Practice

Questions 1-90

41. Mrs. Stevens, a 75-year-old woman with metastatic breast cancer states, "I have so much pain today, I can hardly function. My pain pills just aren't working." Her sister is with her for her visit today. To assess Mrs. Stevens' pain, the nurse should:
    A. Ask her sister to step out of the exam room and ask her more about Mrs. Stevens' pain.
    B. Discuss the pain management plan with Mrs. Stevens.
    C. Give short-acting morphine because she is having pain today.
    D. Have Mrs. Stevens rate the intensity of her pain on a numerical scale and describe the characteristics.

42. The triage nurse receives a call from Mr. Jacobs, a 36-year-old with severe lower back pain. Which of the following indicates he needs to be seen by a provider urgently?
    A. He is out of work on worker's compensation.
    B. He has pain at rest and with movement.
    C. He also has a headache.
    D. He is having trouble with his balance.

43. Desired goals of moderate sedation include which of the following?
    A. Relaxation and loss of reflex response
    B. Respiratory depression and relief of moderate pain
    C. Minimal variation of vital signs and amnesia and/or analgesia
    D. Alternation of mood and minor hypotension

44. Mr. Barnett, 80 years old, calls the office, stating he is depressed and does not feel like living anymore since his wife died a few months ago. The best response from the telehealth nurse would be:
    A. "Perhaps you should come in and see Dr. Green for an appointment later today."
    B. "Mr. Barnett, do you have family living nearby?"
    C. "Mr. Barnett, have you been thinking of killing yourself?"
    D. "Have you had trouble sleeping since your wife passed away?"

45. A 22-year-old female patient has asked the nurse about starting to take St. John's Wort for depression. After ruling out suicidal ideation, which of the following would be the best advice to offer?
    A. St. John's Wort has not been shown to be effective in treating depression.
    B. If one takes St. John's Wort, he or she needs to avoid foods containing high levels of tyramine, such as wine, cheese, and pickles.
    C. For a patient this age, it is most likely premenstrual dysphoric disorder (PMDD) and she should get relief from OTC products.
    D. She needs to speak with her primary care provider about all her medications, since St. John's Wort may interact with other medications such as antidepressants and oral contraceptives.

46. A nurse in ambulatory care should do a physical assessment of a patient's chest in the following order:
    A. Auscultation, inspection, use of accessory muscles, and peripheral perfusion.
    B. Respiratory rate, auscultation, percussion, and forced expiratory volume.
    C. Inspection, palpation, percussion, and auscultation.
    D. Respiratory rate, oxygen saturation by pulse oximetry, inspection, and auscultation.

47. Mrs. Huff, age 27, came to clinic today to see Dr. Williams with a complaint of a sprained shoulder. She has had several clinic visits over the past year for injuries. The nurse notices a bruise on Mrs. Huff's cheek and then notes another on her forearm while taking vital signs. Mrs. Huff says she hurt her shoulder carrying a laundry basket. Mrs. Huff's husband accompanied her today for her clinic appointment. Suspecting domestic violence, the nurse should:
    A. Contact the police to get a statement from Mrs. Huff.
    B. Make a referral to a social worker to help Mrs. Huff find resources she may need.
    C. Ensure Mrs. Huff is examined and interviewed in private.
    D. Discuss her concerns and suspicions with Mr. and Mrs. Huff, and offer to help them find resources to improve their relationship.

Clinical Practice — Questions 1-90

48. Autism spectrum disorder is usually not diagnosed until after age 4. As a nurse in the pediatric primary care office, you know that autism is characterized by:
    A. High-pitched crying.
    B. A 4-year-old unable to write letters and numbers.
    C. A 4-year-old wanting to play with other children and pretend play.
    D. Exhibiting repetitive movements and discomfort with changes in routine.

49. Which of the following developmental milestones should the nurse expect to see in a 12-month old child?
    A. Walks up steps and says six words.
    B. Balances on one foot and towers four blocks.
    C. Throws a ball overhand and drinks from a cup.
    D. Waves bye-bye and stands alone.

50. Which of the following would be found in an adult patient diagnosed with obesity?
    A. A waist-to-hip ratio greater than 2.0 (abdominal girth ÷ hip circumference)
    B. A body mass index greater than or equal to 30
    C. A weight greater than 50th percentile of adults with the same height according to standard life insurance tables
    D. Body weight greater than 100% of ideal body weight

51. How many doses of measles, mumps, and rubella combined vaccine (MMR) should children receive before age 7 years?
    A. 2
    B. 3
    C. 4
    D. 5

52. Which of the following would indicate the need for an emergent evaluation of a child with vomiting and diarrhea?
    A. Fever of 100.6° F in a 4-year-old
    B. Watery stools for 24 hours in a 2-year-old
    C. Recent travel outside the United States
    D. No urine output for 8 hours

53. Which of the following would be commonly recommended for treatment of mild upper-respiratory infection in a child under 6 years old?
    A. Initiate a course of broad-spectrum antibiotics.
    B. Administer over-the-counter cough and cold medications.
    C. Call or make appointment for cough lasting more than 3 days.
    D. Administer acetaminophen or ibuprofen for fever or pain.

54. In a person with human immunodeficiency virus (HIV), the progression to acquired immune deficiency syndrome (AIDS) is defined by which of the following:
    A. Positive enzyme-linked immunosorbent assay (ELISA) and a confirmatory Western Blot.
    B. Nadir CD4+ T cell count and diagnosis of opportunistic condition.
    C. Acute mononucleosis-like symptoms such as fever, malaise, fatigue, body aches, headache, and sore throat.
    D. Continued high-risk sexual behaviors such as condom-less sex with a known HIV+ partner, exchanging sex for drugs, or sex with multiple partners.

55. Which of the following statements by the nurse demonstrates accurate understanding of influenza vaccinations?
    A. Live attenuated influenza vaccine (LAIV) administered intranasally is an option for all children.
    B. First-time vaccines in children 6 months through 8 years should include two doses, 4 weeks apart.
    C. A child with asthma should not receive an influenza vaccination
    D. A pregnant woman would be able to receive intranasal LAIV.

56. A nurse performing telephone triage determines the nature and urgency of the patient's problem using clinical reasoning, tapping their knowledge and experience. This is an example of which component of the telehealth nursing process?
    A. Assessment
    B. Diagnosis
    C. Intervention
    D. Outcomes

57. Which of the following is an example of *wellness bias*, a clinical peril in telehealth nursing practice?
    A. The nurse only gathers assessment information from a spouse who calls to report her husband's symptoms.
    B. A nurse uses decision support tools to improve safety and guide the nursing process in telephone triage in addition to clinical judgment.
    C. The nurse defers a full assessment after a patient calls with self-diagnosis of indigestion because she thinks this is most probable.
    D. A nurse gathers further positive and negative assessment data from a patient who calls with a self-diagnosis of a migraine headache.

Clinical Practice

Questions 1-90

58. Nurses in a surgical clinic are concerned that patients are not following presurgical instructions. There has been a trend of patients eating and drinking too close to the time of their surgical procedure resulting in cancellation. Which of the following describes an evidence-based approach the nurses can explore to improve patient understanding?
    A. Identify patients who followed instructions and interview them to determine success factors.
    B. Review and evaluate research articles about preoperative teaching.
    C. Implement a process to call the patients after preoperative instruction is given to determine their understanding.
    D. Evaluate preoperative teaching materials for language level and revise materials for readability at the 5th grade level.

59. Which of the following is an example of secondary prevention?
    A. Screening colonoscopy at age 45
    B. Human papillomavirus (HPV) vaccination in an 11-year-old
    C. Wearing a seatbelt
    D. Nutritional counseling for patient with diabetes mellitus

60. All of the following are examples of tertiary prevention *except:*
    A. Utilizing the teach-back method by having a patient with diabetes mellitus explain the management of a hypoglycemic event.
    B. Instructing a patient with chronic heart failure to perform home weight monitoring.
    C. Reviewing the cancer screening recommendations at a 50-year-old patient's wellness visit.
    D. Evaluating caregiver understanding of swallowing precautions after their spouse had a stroke with existing dysphagia.

61. Which of the following would *not* demonstrate best practice for assessment of depression for a teenager during a wellness visit?
    A. Utilizing evidence-based depression screening questionnaires.
    B. Inquiring if a teen with depression has had any thoughts of suicide or suicide attempts.
    C. Assessing for common symptoms of depression such as withdrawal from usual social activities.
    D. Conducting the complete assessment with parents present.

62. Which of the following statements by the patient indicates understanding of instructions for management of hypoglycemic episodes?
    A. "If I pass out, my wife can put something with sugar in my mouth."
    B. "I only need to monitor my blood glucose if I have symptoms."
    C. "If my blood glucose is less than 70 mg/dL, I should have 4 ounces of juice and repeat the reading in 15 minutes."
    D. "I won't have a hypoglycemic event if I have type 2 diabetes; that happens with type 1."

63. The goal of the nurse caring for a patient having surgery or a procedure is to:
    A. Clearly recognize different levels of sedation.
    B. Maintain safety and physiologic integrity of the patient.
    C. Provide family members with emotional support.
    D. Coordinate the care team during procedures.

64. Which of the following is an important consideration when determining if a surgical procedure should be performed in an inpatient or ambulatory setting?
    A. Presence of chronic conditions
    B. Procedural requirement for moderate sedation
    C. Urgency of procedure
    D. Postoperative care requirements

65. The primary reason a gastrointestinal (GI) prep is used the day before an abdominal procedure is to:
    A. Improve visualization of upper GI tract.
    B. Minimize patient discomfort.
    C. Improve visualization of the lower GI tract.
    D. Minimize time of procedure.

66. During a preoperative nursing assessment, which finding might result in the cancellation of a scheduled procedure?
    A. Fever
    B. Weight loss
    C. Recent diarrhea
    D. Elevated blood glucose

67. Sources of authoritative statements and standards for provision of moderate sedation in the ambulatory setting include:
    A. American Academy of Ambulatory Care Nursing.
    B. American Nurses Association.
    C. State Board of Nursing.
    D. The Department of Health and Human Services.

Clinical Practice

Questions 1-90

68. Which of the following measures might be included in the patient's postoperative instructions to aid in the prevention of respiratory complications?
    A. Use of vascular compression devices
    B. Use of incentive spirometer
    C. Over-the-counter multivitamin
    D. Use of patient-controlled analgesia pump

69. The postoperative period begins when the patient enters the Post Anesthesia Care Unit (PACU) and ends:
    A. At discharge.
    B. Upon arrival home.
    C. When healing is complete.
    D. When released by primary provider.

70. Prior to the administration of palliative sedation, the following guidelines should be established **except:**
    A. Death should be imminent and expected within days or hours.
    B. Patient or caregiver should be educated on the expectations and goals of sedation.
    C. A do-not-resuscitate order must be in place; however, hydration and other life prolonging therapies may continue.
    D. There is confirmation the patient is gravely suffering.

71. Which of the following pharmacologic options may be helpful in addressing anorexia in terminally ill adults?
    A. Corticosteroids, cannabinoids, and progestational agents
    B. Benzodiazepines, opioids, and metoclopromide
    C. Benzphetamine, phentermine, and cannabinoids
    D. Corticosteroids, pegfilgrastim, and cannabinoids

Questions 72 and 73 pertain to the same scenario.

72. Mr. Peterson is a 74-year-old patient with stage IV lung cancer that has metastasized to the bone. In assessing Mr. Peterson, the nurse should be aware of possible barriers to adequate pain management which include:
    A. Resignation that he has terminal cancer and that nothing helps and nothing can be done.
    B. His health care team is open to homeopathic remedies.
    C. Mr. Peterson's refusal to accept that complete pain relief is unrealistic considering his prognosis.
    D. His use of prayer to help him forget about his pain.

73. Mr. Peterson starts to question the meaning of his life and the contribution to society he has made. The nurse recognizes there needs to be further investigation and discussion of his feelings. This sense of helplessness, hopelessness, meaninglessness, regret, and fear in patients at the end of life may be an indication of:
    A. Anxiety and agitation.
    B. Emotional incapacitation.
    C. Spiritual distress.
    D. Existential distress.

74. A terminally ill patient may experience nociceptive pain which is described as:
    A. A sensation of burning, tingling, or radiating electrical currents.
    B. Throbbing, aching, spastic, and cramping.
    C. Usually chronic and less responsive to opioid drugs.
    D. Perceived pain.

75. The following are benefits of early palliative care referrals **except:**
    A. It allows time to establish and repair relationships between patient and family.
    B. It facilitates immediate discussions about the process of death and dying.
    C. Patients referred early to palliative care have fewer emergency visits and hospitalizations.
    D. Early palliative care has been shown to increase patient and caregiver satisfaction.

76. CRIES is a validated and acceptable tool for assessing pain in patients less than 3 years of age. CRIES stands for:
    A. Crying, Restless, Irritable, Emotional, Sad.
    B. Crying, Requires oxygen for saturation below 95%, Increased vital signs, Expression, and Sleeplessness.
    C. Crying, Restless, Inconsolable, Eating less, Somber.
    D. Crying, Respiratory rate, Inconsolable, Emotional, Sleepy.

77. The nurse can help terminally ill patients who may become despondent and withdrawn by:
    A. Suggesting options for the family to assist with distraction.
    B. Providing information about how other patients have coped with terminal illness.
    C. Recommending a reduction in pain medication to increase engagement with family.
    D. Encouraging grief counseling consistent with patient wishes.

Clinical Practice — Questions 1-90

78. Mrs. James, a 43-year-old patient in the clinic, was recently diagnosed with rheumatoid arthritis. Her current symptoms include fatigue, mild pain, and stiffness in her fingers, especially in the morning. Her treatment goals include which of the following?
    A. Remission, avoiding joint and organ damage, and avoiding disability
    B. Preparation for joint replacement surgery which will likely be required in the next year
    C. Annual medical visits since her symptoms are mild
    D. Medication adherence, reducing physical activity, and annual medical visits

79. Rheumatoid arthritis is more commonly seen in:
    A. Elderly, thin, Caucasian women.
    B. Middle-aged women.
    C. Middle-aged Caucasian men.
    D. Asian women, usually over the age of 55.

80. Which of the following are appropriate treatments for patients with dementia?
    A. Exercise, music, cognitive, and behavioral therapies
    B. Home evaluation to assess for safety of appliances and presence of smoke detectors
    C. Referral to caregiver support resources
    D. Use of alternative therapies such as herbal remedies shown to be effective with dementia

81. Dementia care strategies that include providing warm, soft textures; using smooth, slow movements; and remaining in the patient's central field of vision are especially important in what stage of dementia?
    A. Mild
    B. Moderate
    C. Late
    D. End-stage

82. Which of the following elements is *not* a core dimension of the RN Care Coordination and Transition Management (CCTM®) role?
    A. Advocacy
    B. Spiritual care
    C. Population health management
    D. Patient-centered care planning

83. Mrs. Smith is being dismissed from the hospital setting. She continues to struggle with management of COPD and has no family living nearby. Which of the following would *not* be considered typical transitional care services?
    A. The nurse plans to work with Mrs. Smith over the next year to help her better manage her condition.
    B. The nurse reaches out to Mrs. Smith while in the hospital to let her know of transitional care services.
    C. The nurse coaches Mrs. Smith in how to more effectively self-manage.
    D. The nurse helps the patient identify community resources that may be beneficial in her care.

84. John, an RN CCTM in a primary care practice, is working with Tara, a 5-year-old patient with severe asthma. John is frustrated because Tara has missed her last two appointments. John is concerned about Tara's well-being. What is the *best* response John should make in this situation?
    A. John does nothing and follows his clinic's policy that after two "no-shows" no further appointments are made until the patient reaches out.
    B. John reviews the electronic health record (EHR) to make sure Tara's family was aware of the appointments.
    C. John reviews the EHR and notes that Tara's primary caregiver works day shift at the local nursing home.
    D. John uses multiple ways to reach out such as portal and phone to check on Tara's status and identify appointment barriers.

85. Maria is an RN CCTM providing transition services utilizing the Care Transitions Intervention (CTI) model. Which of the following actions by Maria would be most consistent with application of the CTI model?
    A. Offers to set up medications to ensure adherence to the plan.
    B. Sends a portal message to a patient to set up a clinic appointment.
    C. Sets up home health services if needed for the patient.
    D. Works with the patient to develop a plan of action if symptoms worsen.

Clinical Practice — Questions 1-90

86. Which of the following describes effective outcome statements applying SMART criteria?
    A. Specific, Medical, Appropriate, Relevant, Tangible
    B. Short-term, Measurable, Appropriate, Relevant, Tangible
    C. Specific, Measurable, Attainable, Realistic, Time bound
    D. Selective, Medical, Achievable, Responsive, Thorough

87. What document(s) primarily defines the regulatory standards of telehealth nursing practice?
    A. The American Nurses Association's (ANA's) general nursing practice standards
    B. Scope and Standards of Practice for Professional Telehealth Nursing
    C. State nurse practice acts
    D. Regulatory agency standards, including the Joint Commission, ADA, and OSHA

88. Which of the following point of care tests is *not* routinely performed in ambulatory care settings?
    A. Glucose
    B. Rapid Antigen Detection Strep Test (RADT)
    C. International Normalized Ratio (INR)
    D. Chemistry panel

89. Which of the following actions would demonstrate application of USPSTF recommendations for lead screening?
    A. The RN ensures elevated lead levels are reported to the state health department.
    B. Adult patients complaining of generalized malaise should be screened for blood lead levels.
    C. The RN would do a comprehensive assessment of home environment at all well-child exams.
    D. High-risk children aged 5-9 should be screened for lead levels.

90. The wife of a 60-year-old patient who has a diagnosis of chronic kidney disease contacts the nephrology practice for advice about her husband's symptoms. After checking the release of information to discuss her husband's care, which of the following would prompt the nurse to recommend urgent care?
    A. "My husband has been urinating 10-12 times a day the past few days."
    B. "After the last doctor visit, I noticed that my husband's serum calcium and phosphate are elevated."
    C. "My husband seems confused today."
    D. "Today when I helped my husband check his glucose, I noticed that it was 139 mg/dl."

Communication — Questions 91-129

91. A 60-year-old female patient with no history of chronic illness, telephones the nurse and states: "I just don't feel right today." Which of the following would be the **best** response?
    A. Tell her that since it is difficult to evaluate the problem she should call back if her symptoms become more specific.
    B. Ask the patient for more information, listening for urgent concerns.
    C. Contact her primary care provider for advice.
    D. Suggest she visit a nearby urgent care center for evaluation.

92. Which of the following is a factor in making communication difficult at the end of life?
    A. Most families have a plan for providing for the needs of their dying family member.
    B. Providing comprehensive information is important in the early stages after terminal diagnosis.
    C. The patient's condition may affect his or her cognition and sensory functioning.
    D. The palliative care plan is developed by the interprofessional team and shared with the patient and family at their literacy level.

Communication — Questions 91-129

93. Which of the following would *most* likely result in a communication barrier for a nurse working with a patient who is terminally ill?
    A. Avoidance of difficult topics by the nurse due to fear of expressing emotion.
    B. Lack of knowledge about the medical management options for the patient.
    C. Helping the patient understand that nothing else can be done in their care.
    D. Concerns about patient request for additional opioids for pain control.

94. Which of the following nurse actions would encourage meaningful conversation with a patient?
    A. Avoiding pauses in the conversation and filling silences with words of encouragement.
    B. Encouraging the patient and family to participate in decision-making to the extent they choose.
    C. Focusing on treatment of the disease and the current symptoms.
    D. Utilizing a clinical care guideline for treatment of the primary diagnosis.

95. Which of the following is true related to the care of terminally ill children?
    A. The nurse should avoid direct communication with the child about their illness.
    B. The child usually knows they have a terminal illness even if not told directly.
    C. The other children in the family will naturally reduce family demands in response to a terminally ill sibling.
    D. In the child's presence, the nurse should use words the child does not understand to discuss the child's treatment.

96. A cardiology office has implemented interactive voice recognition technology (IVRT) to monitor the status of patients with chronic heart failure (CHF). The patients receive calls from the IVRT system weekly to solicit data about their weight, ease of breathing, and other indicators. Which of the following is the *most* important feature of the IVRT system?
    A. Menu options should guide the patient through a complex set of responses to solicit detail when there is a positive finding.
    B. Data need to be downloaded and analyzed by the licensed provider who manages the patient's CHF.
    C. The IVRT system needs to allow for a referral to a human resource when needed.
    D. The IVRT system should download data directly into an EHR to be integrated with data from face-to-face encounters.

97. Which of the following is true about telehealth communication between nurses and patients or the patients' caregivers? The nurse:
    A. Should avoid use of self-disclosure to elicit additional information.
    B. Should always use open-ended questions.
    C. Is interpreting the caller's description of symptoms, location, and appearance.
    D. Is employing auditory, tactile, and visual senses to obtain information from the caller.

98. In evaluating Internet information for patient education, which of the following criteria are consistent with the AAACN metric?
    A. Accuracy, Authorship, Attribution, Currency, and Nursing practice relevance
    B. Literacy level, ease of search, endorsement by specialty organizations, and attractive layout
    C. Specificity, outcome oriented, free of abbreviations, and comprehensiveness
    D. Specific, measurable, attainable, relevant, and time-bound

99. Two weeks ago, a 60-year-old female patient was prescribed a diuretic for her newly diagnosed hypertension. She comes to the clinic today for a BP check. The physician's plan of care included adding a beta blocker at the next visit if she has not achieved BP control. With repeated measurement, her BP today is 164/100 mmHg. What action should the nurse take *first*?
    A. Order an ECG and prepare to refer to the emergency room.
    B. Ask the patient if there are barriers for her taking her current medication every day.
    C. Ask directly about her lack of motivation to change her self-care behaviors.
    D. Contact the physician about proceeding with the plan to add a beta blocker.

100. The nursing supervisor of a family medicine office is involved in a major change in the clinic in which RNs will be accountable for developing care plans and managing outcomes for a specific group of patients assigned to each nurse. Which technique would be most appropriate initially in leading this change process?
     A. Hire a nurse consultant to act as expert change agent.
     B. Provide information about financial rewards that may be enjoyed if the change is successful.
     C. Involve the nurses in the planning stages.
     D. Educate the nurses on how to provide care in the new model.

Communication Questions 91-129

101. Which activity would require ambulatory care nurses to apply critical thinking?
   A. Analyzing information in development of a diagnosis and plan of care.
   B. Documenting data to communicate with other health care professionals.
   C. Measuring a patient's vital signs, height, and weight in preparation for a visit with a provider.
   D. Providing normal health screening test results to a healthy patient.

102. Which of the following would be an important strategy to improve one's cultural knowledge and skill?
   A. Explore one's own cultural biases toward people from different cultures.
   B. Reinforce that patients comply with the plan of care regardless of cultural influences.
   C. Focus one's consideration of cultural differences on immigrants, minorities, and marginalized populations.
   D. Attempt to adopt the cultural beliefs and values of the predominant culture groups in the geographic area to the practice setting.

103. John is the nurse collaborating with a geriatrician in the care of a complex patient. During the visit, John documents vital signs, home medications, allergies, and the patient education provided. The geriatrician documents her own assessment data, clinical decision-making, recommendations, and plan of care. One of the most important reasons for detailed nursing documentation is to:
   A. Identify nursing diagnoses.
   B. Support surveillance of reportable diagnoses to authorities.
   C. Satisfy standards of regulatory agencies, such as The Joint Commission.
   D. Communicate observations and care provided to the team and support continuity.

104. A nurse observes a medical assistant calling an elderly patient from the waiting room by his first name. What action should the nurse take?
   A. Apologize to the patient.
   B. Pull the medical assistant aside before calling the next patient and explain why the clinic's customer service standards require a different approach.
   C. Report the poor customer service behavior to the medical assistant's supervisor to provide feedback and corrective intervention.
   D. Pull the medical assistant aside before calling the next patient and inform them to never address a patient so casually.

105. In times of stress, communication between health care providers and patients and families can be more challenging. In this context, which of the following is true?
   A. Conflict between health care team and patient is expected and an external third party should be engaged early.
   B. When discussing concerns with the patient and family, consider both their current and past concerns together.
   C. Assess for expressions of excessive anger that would indicate the presence of conflict.
   D. If the family calls frequently with concerns, it is better to wait a day or two to respond to limit communication.

106. When transitioning a patient's care from one health care provider to another, effective handoff communication is supported by:
   A. Useing a structured, comprehensive tool or model.
   B. Limiting the handoff report to critical physiologic data.
   C. Providing information to patient/family to relay to next care provider.
   D. Utilizing the situation, background, analysis of problems, and recommendations (SBAR) approach.

107. The Nursing Minimum Data Set (NMDS) includes:
   A. Living arrangements of the patient, names of significant others, race and ethnicity, country of birth.
   B. Date of birth of patient, RN provider, admissions or encounter data, nursing care elements.
   C. Patient disposition, race and ethnicity, facility information, names of significant others.
   D. Country of birth, race and ethnicity, patient demographics, nursing care elements.

108. Which of the following might indicate a barrier in an individual's physical readiness to learn?
   A. Hearing impairment
   B. High level of anxiety
   C. Lack of pre-existing knowledge of the topic
   D. Language difference in the absence of an interpreter

Communication

Questions 91-129

109. Mrs. Jackson called today because her adolescent son is developing some blemishes and she wants to learn more about acne. The nurse responds that she will mail some printed materials for Mrs. Jackson to read. What is a possible disadvantage of providing printed materials to Mrs. Jackson?
    A. Printed materials tend to decrease retention of the information.
    B. Printed materials limit the interaction to determine understanding and specific needs.
    C. The materials may be used by others who are not the intended audience.
    D. Reading printed material increases the time demand of the learner over other instructional methods.

110. Which of the following is a method for providing performance metrics to consumers?
    A. Publishing clinical care guidelines, such as on the National Guideline Clearinghouse.
    B. Applying nationally recognized processes for quality improvement such as Six Sigma or Lean.
    C. Releasing report cards that contain data about important indicators of care.
    D. Filing sentinel event reports with The Joint Commission.

111. Which of the following would reflect appropriate communication skills used in telehealth nursing?
    A. Utilizing a decision support tool, such as an algorithm, to guide the questions asked of the caller.
    B. Electronically recording the call for purposes of risk management and quality improvement.
    C. Clarifying the reason the patient is calling and listening intently to the information.
    D. Encouraging the patient to self-diagnose and/or indicate the treatment he or she is seeking.

112. In practices in which the nurse has frequent encounters with a patient over a long period of time, maintaining professional boundaries can be challenging. Which example demonstrates healthy professional boundaries?
    A. The patient needs help with getting some work done on her car. Her lack of transportation is interfering with getting to appointments. The RN locates a repair shop nearby and offers to take her car to it.
    B. The nurse discloses she is having financial difficulties at home and says she may have to change jobs.
    C. The patient surprises the nurse with a broach that has been in the family for years. The nurse expresses gratitude for the thoughtful gift.
    D. The nurse lets the patient know that she will be her RN Care Coordinator for approximately 6 months.

113. According to the Transtheoretical Model of Change, which of the following statements reflects a patient who is in the contemplation stage?
    A. "I think I will be able to begin exercising next month after the weather gets a little warmer."
    B. "I will be able to lose weight next year after I cut back to part-time hours."
    C. "I routinely exercise on Monday, Thursday, and Saturday."
    D. "I feel confident I will be able to keep up my new routine."

114. What is an example of an action a nurse could take to improve communication if uncertain about gender identity?
    A. Take cues from patient appearance to determine how to address the patient.
    B. Use EHR demographic information to address patient, as it is the most updated.
    C. Review the EHR to determine birth gender.
    D. Ask the patient how they would like to be addressed.

115. The nurse manager demonstrates excellent communication skills related to emergency preparedness by:
    A. Ensuring competencies are assessed annually.
    B. Planning regular drills to test performance.
    C. Debriefing staff after each drill and discussing opportunities for improvement.
    D. Ensuring alternative plans for communication are in place if systems fail.

Communication

Questions 91-129

116. Empathic communication skills can help improve communication during difficult conversations. What statement **best** reflects use of empathic communication skills?
    A. "I am sorry you have waited so long for your immunization. We are short staffed, and I got here as soon as I could."
    B. "I am giving you your pain medications as soon as I can, are you sure you are still uncomfortable?"
    C. "Dr. Jones has not answered my page yet, so I don't know if you will be able to go home today."
    D. "Thank you for sharing your frustration about waiting. I understand it must have been hard for you to wait and I am sorry. Now that I am here what can I do to help you?"

117. Customer service is **best** described as the:
    A. Ability to meet and manage customer expectations.
    B. Ability to communicate effectively with patients.
    C. Using specific techniques to respond to patient complaints.
    D. Development of specific guidelines staff can use to address customer concerns.

118. A patient is on the phone and the front desk indicated that she is very angry. She indicates she asked for information and what she received was useless. The nurse checks the record quickly and notes that a patient education brochure about diabetes was mailed to the patient last week. What should the nurse's best response be?
    A. "Did you receive the brochure I mailed you last week?"
    B. "I can make an appointment with your physician assistant next week if that is OK."
    C. "Are you having difficulty reading the brochure?"
    D. "I am sorry the brochure was not helpful. Can you share more with me about your concerns?"

119. The nurse enters the exam room to take a patient's vitals and finds she is very angry and shouting. The nurse recognizes the situation could get out of hand and identifies the need for de-escalation. The nurse is worried that he will not be able to stay in control. What technique would be the best for the nurse to employ?
    A. Demonstrate caring by touching the patient's shoulder softly.
    B. Ask the patient to lower her voice as it is not appropriate in the clinic.
    C. Approach the patient calmly but remain near the door in case exit is needed.
    D. Be very firm and directive in approaching the patient.

120. Mr. Brown is very upset about how long he has waited for his appointment with his physician. What initial action would be consistent with principles of service recovery?
    A. Discuss the patient's concerns with the registration staff and reschedule the appointment.
    B. Let him know you will inform the manager and provide a small token or gesture as available in service recovery guidelines.
    C. Apologize for the delay, invite him to call customer service and provide the phone number.
    D. Acknowledge the delay, let him know his provider will be available in 10 minutes, and ask what he would like to do.

121. When checking the emergency cart's defibrillator, the nurse finds it fails to charge rapidly to the appropriate level. In contacting the equipment maintenance department, she learns there have been similar issues with several defibrillators in the facility. After assuring well-functioning equipment is in place in the immediate patient care area, what is the most important action the nurse should take next?
    A. Assure a report is submitted to the manufacturer and the Food and Drug Administration regarding the equipment failure.
    B. Negotiate with the manufacturer for replacement or reimbursement for the defective equipment.
    C. Work with the nurse manager and biomedical department to develop a plan to assess all defibrillators in the facility for potential failure and communicate concerns.
    D. Reassess the number of defibrillators and other types of emergency equipment that need to be available for patient emergencies across the facility.

122. One of the developmental considerations for teaching an adolescent is:
    A. They tend to build on past life experiences which may be relevant to the new learning.
    B. They may reflect on unsatisfactory life aspects and need reinforcement of their own abilities to modify them.
    C. When self-identity is threatened, autonomy can be supported by involving them in decision-making whenever possible.
    D. Parents are strong role models for the development of health habits at this stage and should be involved.

Communication

Questions 91-129

123. Nurses working in a preoperative setting practice effective communication when they:
    A. Determine the patient's adherence to preoperative instructions.
    B. Initiate post-procedural referrals as needed.
    C. Ensure the patient has arranged for a ride home after the procedure.
    D. Discuss the importance of fall risk procedures after administration of preoperative medications.

124. A nurse is practicing in an ambulatory care setting and her colleague practices in an inpatient setting. The inpatient nurse would like to know more about ambulatory care nursing. The ambulatory care nurse references the Standards of Practice for Professional Ambulatory Care Nursing. Which statement identifies Standards of Professional Performance for ambulatory care nurses?
    A. Nursing process, health teaching, telehealth, and environment
    B. Nursing process, research and evidence-based practice, collaboration
    C. Telehealth, leadership, consultation
    D. Ethics, education, communication, professional practice evaluation

125. An example of a SMART goal would include:
    A. Walk to the mailbox and back three times per week for the next 4 weeks.
    B. Develop a COPD action plan to improve respiratory function over the next 4-6 months.
    C. Adopt DASH diet guidelines, check BP frequently, call clinic if BP is elevated.
    D. Take medications as prescribed, report symptoms, check blood glucose at least daily.

126. Which of the following is a statement consistent with application of motivational interviewing used to improve interaction among team members?
    A. "How might things be different if you…"
    B. "It would be helpful to set SMART goals to assure success of this project."
    C. "You might want to consider more self-awareness in interactions with the team."
    D. "We should start by creating a safe environment to have a frank discussion between colleagues."

127. Which statement is consistent with positive communication for staff retention?
    A. "Our unit is not performing well in our hand hygiene measures, so starting tomorrow, please report any colleagues to me who are observed not performing handwashing according to procedure."
    B. "We have had some instances in which we have had new staff turnover after hiring. What are we doing wrong that seems to be turning new staff away?"
    C. "Because our unit is having budget issues, we will need to shorten the length of orientation of new graduates to 3 months."
    D. "Our organization is considering starting a nurse residency program for new graduate nurses. I am looking for volunteers to serve on the design team."

128. Many factors influence the need to recruit new nursing staff. Which of the following is *not* one of the factors?
    A. The average age of nurses in the United States is approximately 53 years.
    B. Projected faculty turnover
    C. Regional variation
    D. Compensation

129. Nursing documentation assists to support which of the following purposes of the medical record:
    A. Provides credible evidence of proof of care given.
    B. Establishes liability for nursing care omissions.
    C. Demonstrates the nurse's clinical reasoning and decision-making.
    D. Points out clinical errors or gaps.

Professional Role

Questions 130-140

130. If a telehealth nurse, licensed and practicing in Wisconsin, is providing telephone care to a patient in Arizona, which of the following is true?
    A. The care is being delivered in Wisconsin, where the nurse is on the phone, so the Wisconsin license is sufficient.
    B. If both Wisconsin and Arizona participate in the interstate Nurse Licensure Compact (NLC), the nurse may deliver nursing care in Arizona within that state's scope of practice.
    C. No nursing care can be delivered over any state boundaries, so the patient needs to seek care in the state where they are physically located.
    D. If both Wisconsin and Arizona participate in the NLC, the nurse must submit their license and other information to Arizona for endorsement.

131. Federal and state laws require public health reporting in which of the following situations?
    A. Fraudulent billing claims
    B. Diagnosis of a serious communicable disease
    C. Employment discrimination based on race, color, religion, sex, or national origin
    D. Malpractice claims against a licensed professional

132. The purpose of a rating system for levels of evidence in evidence-based practice (EBP) guidelines is to:
    A. Indicate the optimal treatment plan that promotes the best patient outcomes.
    B. Allow the reviewer to estimate the quality and strength of the evidence.
    C. Enhance the adoption of best practices.
    D. Demonstrate the strength of the link to national standards.

133. Which of the following is true about EBP?
    A. Relies on established clinical practices from within an organization and the personal experiences of clinicians as the basis for designing practice standards.
    B. Integrates research evidence with clinical experience to support the best recommended guideline for evidence.
    C. Best evidence comes from systematic reviews of qualitative studies.
    D. Measures the outcomes or results of care.

134. The Enhanced Nurse Licensure Compact (eNLC) differs from the NLC in that:
    A. It allows for standard scope of practice in all eNLC states.
    B. It has been operational for at least 15 years.
    C. It requires all states in which an RN is practicing to conduct background checks.
    D. It allows for telehealth nursing practice across eNLC states without additional licenses.

135. Nursing practice standards exist to:
    A. Serve as a guide for the structure and processes in the delivery of nursing care.
    B. Describe legally mandated requirements for competent patient care.
    C. Outline consumer-directed expectations for care delivery.
    D. Promote nursing care delivery in the hospital and ambulatory care setting.

136. The ANA *Code of Ethics* provides that:
    A. Nursing educational programs have the same core curricula.
    B. The regulation of the practice of nursing by state practice acts does not vary widely from state to state.
    C. Professional nurses will administer patient care with compassion.
    D. The title *registered nurse* is protected and may only be used by those meeting the licensure requirements.

137. Best practices for the management of chronic pain using opioid therapy do *not* include:
    A. Ensuring availability of naloxone when opioid and benzodiazepine therapy is prescribed.
    B. Establishing mutually agreed upon therapy goals through behavioral contract.
    C. Performing a urine drug screen upon initiation and at least annually.
    D. Educating patients about constipation with chronic opioid use.

138. Which of the following is true about delegation by an RN?
    A. The nurse may delegate aspects of the nursing process.
    B. State practice acts uniformly define the scope of delegation allowed by RNs.
    C. The delegating nurse remains responsible for the delegated task.
    D. The nurse may delegate a task based on another RN's judgment.

Professional Role

Questions 130-140

139. The patient informs the nurse that he wants to stop chemotherapy treatments, but a family member is insistent on continuing treatments. The **first** step of the ethical decision-making models is:
    A. Identify medical facts.
    B. Define the ethical dilemma.
    C. Identify non-medical facts.
    D. Separate assumptions from facts.

140. Non-maleficence refers to the ethical directive to:
    A. Tell the truth under all circumstances.
    B. Avoid doing harm.
    C. Avoid prejudging a patient or situation.
    D. Distribute care equitably.

Systems/Legal and Regulatory

Questions 141-160

141. A goal of performance improvement is to:
    A. Identify root causes of problems and errors.
    B. Validate existing knowledge and generate new knowledge.
    C. Measure and report the health status of patients.
    D. Determine if the desired outcome has been achieved.

142. The group practice is planning renovation of space for a new clinic. When planning for furnishings or equipment, what needs to be considered **first?**
    A. Equipping the unit with safety rails and grab bars for elderly patients.
    B. Identifying population of patients served by the new clinic.
    C. Furnishing lobby areas with appropriately sized furniture for children.
    D. Choosing furnishings that are designed for easy cleaning.

143. Which of the following statements would reflect practice guidelines related to verbal orders?
    A. Verbal orders are not considered safe and in most organizations they are prohibited.
    B. The nurse writes down the order immediately and reads it back for verification.
    C. If the ordering physician is unavailable for authentication, the order can be signed by an advanced practice provider covering the physician.
    D. Advanced practice providers are unable to give verbal orders.

Questions 144-146 pertain to the same scenario.

144. The group practice is purchasing an office building and renovating it for ambulatory care for both family medicine and medical specialties. It is not adjacent to the hospital but is in an area that is considered "low crime" and otherwise safe. From a nursing perspective, which of the following is **most** important regarding the exterior of the building?
    A. Conveniently accessible via public transportation.
    B. Signage at the street is visible and clearly describes the facility.
    C. The parking lot and curbs do not pose fall hazards and allow for wheelchair and stretcher access.
    D. The façade and landscaping are attractive and congruent with the environment.

145. The waiting area for all the specialties is planned for one centralized location, with check-in windows for each clinical unit. Privacy of the check-in and registration areas is supported by partitioning and soundproofing. A play area for children is planned in one cluster of the seating. What other layout issue for the entrance, check-in, and waiting areas would be most important from a nursing perspective?
    A. The space is warm and welcoming.
    B. The patients' entrance is separate from the staff entrance.
    C. There are bulletproof glass enclosures around the cashiers.
    D. There is a separate waiting space for patients with potentially communicable diseases.

Systems/Legal and Regulatory

Questions 141-160

146. Prior to final approval of the space plan, the nurse manager identifies several additional clinical concerns. Which of the following is most important to safe patient care?
    A. Appropriate areas to store, dispose of, or reprocess equipment.
    B. A flag or light system for communicating the status of the exam and treatment rooms.
    C. Standardized exam room layouts.
    D. Space for patient teaching and nursing interventions in close proximity to the telephone workspace.

147. In managing the budget of an outpatient clinic, which of the following would be considered a direct and variable cost of providing patient services?
    A. Rent of the suite of offices and exam rooms
    B. Cost of the human resources department, which manages hiring, payroll, and benefits
    C. Cost of the vaccines and other stock medications
    D. Liability insurance

148. The general surgery physician group is planning to hire a bariatric surgeon to provide surgical interventions for patients who are morbidly obese. Which of the following facilities and equipment changes would be *most* important for staff safety?
    A. Hallway and doorway clearance will accommodate extra-wide wheelchairs.
    B. The area to discharge the patient from the clinic is near the exit of the building.
    C. Patient transfer and lift devices are easily accessible.
    D. Hallway safety rails are installed.

149. The growth in ambulatory care in the past 20 years has been primarily driven by:
    A. Increased payment by Accountable Care Organizations for the use of new technology in outpatient settings.
    B. Changes in reimbursements that have made it more cost effective to provide care in outpatient settings.
    C. Patient preferences to have their care delivered in outpatient settings whenever possible.
    D. Increased demand for services overall, as people are living longer with chronic illness.

150. Which of the following is true about determining staffing in ambulatory care?
    A. Benchmarking surveys provide ratios that are useful in all ambulatory care specialties.
    B. There are several well-researched formulas and tools in the literature for determining staffing in ambulatory care.
    C. Factors that influence staffing include non-visit care volume, types of patient encounters, and requirements for each encounter.
    D. Primary care clinics and surgical specialty clinics have very similar staffing requirements.

151. Which of the following is the standard method of reporting patient services to receive payment from government and private health plans?
    A. Documentation
    B. Coding
    C. Visit numbers
    D. Relative value units

152. The National Committee for Quality Assurance sponsors and maintains Health Plan Employer Data and Information Set (HEDIS®) for which of the following purposes?
    A. Provide a vehicle for peer review of significant utilization abnormalities within managed care provider groups.
    B. Assure purchasers and consumers have the information they need to reliably compare the performance of managed care organizations.
    C. Provide data to prospective employees of managed care organizations and their provider agencies about the safety record of the agency.
    D. Allow data sharing among all the providers who participate in a health plan about health care outcomes for specified diagnoses and interventions.

153. The standard rules and reporting mechanisms for health care services are determined by what section within the U.S. Department of Health and Human Services?
    A. Social Security Administration
    B. Veterans Administration
    C. Agency for Healthcare Research and Quality
    D. Centers for Medicare & Medicaid Services

154. Which of the following describes a fixed payment received by providers of health care services at set intervals for each patient in a health plan for which they are providing care?
    A. Precertification
    B. Indemnity payment
    C. Capitation
    D. Bundled payments

Systems/Legal and Regulatory — Questions 141-160

155. Which of the following falls into the category of a semi-critical item that would require use of high-level disinfection?
    A. An endoscope used for upper gastroenterological procedures
    B. Surgical instruments
    C. An exam table after being contaminated with body substances during a procedure
    D. The electrodes of an electrocardiogram machine

156. The role of institutional ethics committees is to:
    A. Make binding decisions for patients and families in conflict.
    B. Protect the legal liability of institutions.
    C. Educate and provide guidance to health care professionals and other staff.
    D. Represent the ethical stance of the institution to the community at large.

157. Which of the following is true regarding nurses utilizing public social media platforms to anonymously post derogatory remarks about patients or colleagues? Nurses:
    A. Are allowed to do so as long as the colleague or patient remains unidentified, although the place of employment is listed on the profile page.
    B. Should be covered as long as the nurse is not on the clock and does not use last names.
    C. May not be held accountable if the nurse, patient, and employer all remain unidentifiable.
    D. Can do so freely as long as the named patients and colleagues are from a previous employer in another state.

158. A 19-year-old female patient reports to the clinic for complaint of headaches. While interviewing the patient, the nurse notices signs of a healing periorbital hematoma and multiple contusions on each arm. When the nurse asks about them the patient breaks down, crying, and states that they were caused by her boyfriend. The patient requests that this information remain confidential. Which action would be consistent with the Health Insurance Portability and Accountability Act (HIPAA)? The nurse:
    A. Is unable to take any further action, based on patient confidentiality.
    B. Calls the family to discuss concerns.
    C. Calls law enforcement immediately to report the issue.
    D. Reports this information to the appropriate public health authorities.

159. When planning next year's budget, which of the following statements **best** represents important considerations for the ambulatory care nurse leader?
    A. New equipment needs, projected salary increases, historical performance
    B. Closed legal case expenses, projected number of visits, building repairs
    C. New services, current inventory, immunizations in stock
    D. Known physician turnover, historical performance, anticipated DRG changes

160. An advanced beneficiary notice is:
    A. A document signed by a patient indicating requested services may not be covered.
    B. The difference between what is charged and what insurance will pay.
    C. A statement that summarizes what has been billed, what has been reimbursed by Medicare, and what the patient must pay to the provider.
    D. Documents sent annually to beneficiaries describing service coverage.

Education

Questions 161-180

161. *Healthy People 2020* includes an objective that health care providers address health literacy needs by several actions including:
    A. Asking the patient to describe how they will follow the instructions provided.
    B. Facilitating access to specialized health services.
    C. Addressing the patient's emotional readiness to learn.
    D. Providing more written materials and/or Internet resources.

162. A telephone triage RN receives a call from a 45-year-old woman complaining of a "migraine headache." The nurse determines this patient has many knowledge deficits related to headaches and their management. What would be an appropriate rationale for deferring the education to another time?
    A. Migraine headaches are more common in some ethnic minorities, and the nurse is unsure about this woman's ethnic background.
    B. The patient may not be physically or emotionally ready to learn since she is in significant pain.
    C. Patients with migraine headaches need to be seen and evaluated by a provider urgently, so the nurse needs to facilitate an urgent appointment or a visit to the emergency department.
    D. The nurse is unable to provide this patient with the clinic's standard teaching sheet for migraine headaches.

163. Population health management care delivery:
    A. Is a strategy to reduce utilization.
    B. Uses data to design clinical interventions.
    C. Emphasizes the need for specialty teams managing chronic illness.
    D. Primarily targets patient groups who have difficulty engaging in care.

164. Which of the following is cited frequently as a barrier to patient counseling in ambulatory care?
    A. Lack of interest by patients
    B. Time constraints for clinicians and the episodic nature of interactions
    C. Inability to overcome language barriers and low literacy
    D. Lack of community resources and printed materials

165. Motivational interviewing is a technique characterized by:
    A. Patients learning by observing others.
    B. Patients' behavior change in response to reinforcements; increasing rewards for healthy behaviors and decreasing rewards for unhealthy behaviors.
    C. Patients taking health-related action if they perceive illness risk or severity can be reduced by taking action.
    D. Health care providers promoting self-efficacy and guiding patients to evaluate their own behavior and generate their own solutions to change.

166. In providing health education about weight management to a larger group, which instructional method is most likely to be successful?
    A. Case study with handouts
    B. Role playing
    C. PowerPoint presentation and discussion
    D. Simulation exercises

167. Whitney, a 24-year-old African American, just delivered her first baby. She does not want any extra tests done on her baby and does not see the reason for having the baby tested for sickle cell disease, since she and her partner are both healthy. Her nurse would best explain the reason for testing by saying:
    A. One in 10 African Americans has sickle cell trait, and 1 in 325 has sickle cell disease.
    B. Whitney may have sickle cell disease and not know it because the chronic anemia and vaso-occlusive effects of sickle cell disease usually occur when a woman is in labor.
    C. Although she and her partner may be healthy, they may still have sickle cell trait, which could result in disease in their baby.
    D. There are four major variants of the disease, and she or her partner may have one of the milder forms.

Education

Questions 161-180

168. A 53-year-old man has recently been diagnosed with diabetes. The provider has sent him to the nurse for instruction about glucose monitoring at home. The patient arrives for teaching as scheduled but has not yet purchased the electronic monitoring device. Which of the following would be the **best** nursing action at this time?
    A. Assess the patient's current understanding and his interest in learning about self-monitoring his glucose.
    B. Demonstrate the procedure using the glucose-monitoring device used in the office.
    C. Have the office assistant give him written materials about glucose control and schedule him to return another day to discuss.
    D. Spend the time available today teaching about glucose metabolism and diabetes and schedule another visit to teach glucose monitoring.

169. Educating the community about primary prevention of HIV and other sexually transmitted diseases would include the following:
    A. Use of condoms and avoidance of anonymous partners.
    B. Vaccination against herpes, hepatitis, and meningococcal infections.
    C. Prophylactic antibiotics for any oral sex.
    D. Annual health screenings.

170. Which of the following would be consistent with principles of anticipatory guidance?
    A. Assists families in managing acute care crises.
    B. Provides structured education targeted at management of chronic conditions.
    C. Prepares patients or caregivers for expected changes.
    D. Uses population health principles to design interventions for groups of patients.

171. Legal mandates for professional nurses to educate patients include:
    A. The Joint Commission requirements.
    B. State nurse practice acts.
    C. ANA Standards of Practice.
    D. American Hospital Association's list of patient rights.

172. Ms. Brown, a 21-year-old university student, has been diagnosed with hepatitis A. She insists she is able to return to classes. An important aspect of her patient education is:
    A. Hepatitis A is contagious and she needs to take precautions to prevent transmission to others.
    B. Hepatitis A is a reportable disease, so she needs to contact the health department.
    C. She probably contracted this illness because she has not been taking good care of herself, with proper rest and nutrition.
    D. Smoking or secondhand smoke exposure will delay her recovery.

173. What is the **most** important factor to consider in choosing printed materials for patient education?
    A. Age of the patient
    B. Developmental stage of the patient
    C. Patient readiness to learn
    D. Literacy level of the patient

174. Following a breast biopsy under moderate sedation, the nurse is preparing to discharge the patient. What patient education is most important for the patient's safety in the next few hours?
    A. How to take care of the wound and identify signs of infection.
    B. How to obtain the biopsy results.
    C. Eating and drinking lightly until the nausea from the sedation subsides.
    D. Avoiding driving or operating machinery for the rest of the day.

175. If a patient is screened and found to have hypertension and dyslipidemia, what lifestyle recommendations should be considered?
    A. Plan for a screening stress electrocardiogram every 5 years.
    B. Manage weight through diet and exercise.
    C. Avoid constipation through fluids and high-fiber foods to prevent straining to have a bowel movement.
    D. Drink the equivalent of eight glasses of water daily because of the risk of kidney damage.

Education

Questions 161-180

176. Mr. McIntyre, 37 years old, has a 25-pack-year history of smoking. Today, he has told his physician he is ready to quit. The nurse has been asked to assist Mr. McIntyre. Which of the following describes application of motivational interviewing principles to assist this patient to quit smoking?
    A. Explain that relapsing is part of the process.
    B. Advise Mr. McIntyre about the harms of smoking, which impact nearly every organ in his body.
    C. Set specific goals and a quit date.
    D. Help him understand his ambivalence about quitting.

177. Topics important to include in counseling parents of school-aged children about childhood obesity include:
    A. Diets high in energy are also high in nutritional value.
    B. Provide a variety of foods, including grains, fruits, and vegetables.
    C. School-aged children will automatically choose the right nutrients for themselves if they see their parents and other role models doing so.
    D. A multivitamin is important to supplement a child's diet at this age.

178. In counseling parents about childhood or adolescent drinking, which of the following should be considered?
    A. Screening children and adolescents for alcohol use is ineffective.
    B. Parental behaviors impact child or adolescent drinking behaviors.
    C. "Risky" drinking has been defined as more than four drinks per occasion for males and more than three drinks per occasion for females.
    D. Speaking frequently with a child about drinking is likely to alienate them and may have a negative rather than positive effect on behavior.

179. For patients with chronic pain, education interventions should include:
    A. Masking nonverbal indications of pain to reduce the anxiety of the family and other caregivers.
    B. Learning to tolerate mild-to-moderate pain without interventions to avoid pain medications.
    C. Recognizing distraction and relaxation techniques are rarely helpful in reducing pain long-term.
    D. Understanding the length of action of various medications and which can be taken together or alternately.

180. Which of the following describes the evaluation phase of patient education?
    A. Tailoring teaching, learning strategies, and interventions
    B. Measuring learning attained and level of self-efficacy
    C. Determining readiness to learn and learning needs
    D. Mutually setting goals and outcomes expected

Ambulatory Care Nursing Review Questions Answer Sheet   #1-90

1.	A	B	C	D	46.	A	B	C	D
2.	A	B	C	D	47.	A	B	C	D
3.	A	B	C	D	48.	A	B	C	D
4.	A	B	C	D	49.	A	B	C	D
5.	A	B	C	D	50.	A	B	C	D
6.	A	B	C	D	51.	A	B	C	D
7.	A	B	C	D	52.	A	B	C	D
8.	A	B	C	D	53.	A	B	C	D
9.	A	B	C	D	54.	A	B	C	D
10.	A	B	C	D	55.	A	B	C	D
11.	A	B	C	D	56.	A	B	C	D
12.	A	B	C	D	57.	A	B	C	D
13.	A	B	C	D	58.	A	B	C	D
14.	A	B	C	D	59.	A	B	C	D
15.	A	B	C	D	60.	A	B	C	D
16.	A	B	C	D	61.	A	B	C	D
17.	A	B	C	D	62.	A	B	C	D
18.	A	B	C	D	63.	A	B	C	D
19.	A	B	C	D	64.	A	B	C	D
20.	A	B	C	D	65.	A	B	C	D
21.	A	B	C	D	66.	A	B	C	D
22.	A	B	C	D	67.	A	B	C	D
23.	A	B	C	D	68.	A	B	C	D
24.	A	B	C	D	69.	A	B	C	D
25.	A	B	C	D	70.	A	B	C	D
26.	A	B	C	D	71.	A	B	C	D
27.	A	B	C	D	72.	A	B	C	D
28.	A	B	C	D	73.	A	B	C	D
29.	A	B	C	D	74.	A	B	C	D
30.	A	B	C	D	75.	A	B	C	D
31.	A	B	C	D	76.	A	B	C	D
32.	A	B	C	D	77.	A	B	C	D
33.	A	B	C	D	78.	A	B	C	D
34.	A	B	C	D	79.	A	B	C	D
35.	A	B	C	D	80.	A	B	C	D
36.	A	B	C	D	81.	A	B	C	D
37.	A	B	C	D	82.	A	B	C	D
38.	A	B	C	D	83.	A	B	C	D
39.	A	B	C	D	84.	A	B	C	D
40.	A	B	C	D	85.	A	B	C	D
41.	A	B	C	D	86.	A	B	C	D
42.	A	B	C	D	87.	A	B	C	D
43.	A	B	C	D	88.	A	B	C	D
44.	A	B	C	D	89.	A	B	C	D
45.	A	B	C	D	90.	A	B	C	D

Ambulatory Care Nursing Review Questions Answer Sheet #91-180

91.	A	B	C	D		136.	A	B	C	D
92.	A	B	C	D		137.	A	B	C	D
93.	A	B	C	D		138.	A	B	C	D
94.	A	B	C	D		139.	A	B	C	D
95.	A	B	C	D		140.	A	B	C	D
96.	A	B	C	D		141.	A	B	C	D
97.	A	B	C	D		142.	A	B	C	D
98.	A	B	C	D		143.	A	B	C	D
99.	A	B	C	D		144.	A	B	C	D
100.	A	B	C	D		145.	A	B	C	D
101.	A	B	C	D		146.	A	B	C	D
102.	A	B	C	D		147.	A	B	C	D
103.	A	B	C	D		148.	A	B	C	D
104.	A	B	C	D		149.	A	B	C	D
105.	A	B	C	D		150.	A	B	C	D
106.	A	B	C	D		151.	A	B	C	D
107.	A	B	C	D		152.	A	B	C	D
108.	A	B	C	D		153.	A	B	C	D
109.	A	B	C	D		154.	A	B	C	D
110.	A	B	C	D		155.	A	B	C	D
111.	A	B	C	D		156.	A	B	C	D
112.	A	B	C	D		157.	A	B	C	D
113.	A	B	C	D		158.	A	B	C	D
114.	A	B	C	D		159.	A	B	C	D
115.	A	B	C	D		160.	A	B	C	D
116.	A	B	C	D		161.	A	B	C	D
117.	A	B	C	D		162.	A	B	C	D
118.	A	B	C	D		163.	A	B	C	D
119.	A	B	C	D		164.	A	B	C	D
120.	A	B	C	D		165.	A	B	C	D
121.	A	B	C	D		166.	A	B	C	D
122.	A	B	C	D		167.	A	B	C	D
123.	A	B	C	D		168.	A	B	C	D
124.	A	B	C	D		169.	A	B	C	D
125.	A	B	C	D		170.	A	B	C	D
126.	A	B	C	D		171.	A	B	C	D
127.	A	B	C	D		172.	A	B	C	D
128.	A	B	C	D		173.	A	B	C	D
129.	A	B	C	D		174.	A	B	C	D
130.	A	B	C	D		175.	A	B	C	D
131.	A	B	C	D		176.	A	B	C	D
132.	A	B	C	D		177.	A	B	C	D
133.	A	B	C	D		178.	A	B	C	D
134.	A	B	C	D		179.	A	B	C	D
135.	A	B	C	D		180.	A	B	C	D

Answer Key for Ambulatory Care Review Questions #1-90

The rationale for each correct answer is found in the *Core Curriculum for Ambulatory Care Nursing, 4th edition,* on the page indicated.

Clinical Practice

Question	Answer	Page
1.	B	335
2.	C	337
3.	C	339
4.	D	341
5.	A	285 — Key word is "intervention."
6.	B	271
7.	C	291
8.	A	177, 467
9.	B	147, 468
10.	D	151
11.	D	286
12.	B	152
13.	C	283
14.	A	298
15.	A	251
16.	D	254
17.	A	294
18.	A	356
19.	D	60
20.	A	22
21.	B	351
22.	B	381-385
23.	A	115
24.	B	403
25.	C	322
26.	C	332
27.	B	334
28.	B	373-376
29.	C	352
30.	B	424-427
31.	B	424-427
32.	D	260
33.	D	432, 441
34.	B	452
35.	A	354
36.	D	363, 366
37.	D	304
38.	B	88-89
39.	D	315
40.	C	134
41.	D	429
42.	D	283
43.	C	304
44.	C	266
45.	D	267
46.	C	121
47.	C	269
48.	D	415
49.	D	415
50.	B	221
51.	A	245
52.	D	297
53.	D	295
54.	B	344
55.	B	245
56.	B	151
57.	C	154
58.	B	45, 207
59.	A	177
60.	C	177
61.	D	266
62.	C	259
63.	B	308
64.	D	303
65.	C	305
66.	A	306
67.	B	309
68.	B	306
69.	C	311
70.	C	436-437
71.	A	438
72.	A	428
73.	D	429
74.	B	429
75.	B	425
76.	B	435
77.	D	447
78.	A	390
79.	B	389
80.	A	399
81.	D	401
82.	B	188
83.	A	192
84.	D	197
85.	D	193
86.	C	123
87.	C	159 — Key word is "regulatory."
88.	D	129-132
89.	A	243
90.	C	379

Answer Key for Ambulatory Care Review Questions   #91-180

Communication

Question	Answer	Page	
91.	B	155	
92.	C	426	
93.	A	426	
94.	B	427	
95.	B	427	
96.	C	107	
97.	C	155	
98.	A	106	
99.	B	169	
100.	C	40	
101.	A	119	
102.	A	22	
103.	D	103	
104.	B	18	
105.	C	20-21	
106.	A	193	
107.	B	100	
108.	A	167	Key word is "physical."
109.	B	174	
110.	C	214-215	
111.	C	155	
112.	D	18	
113.	A	20	
114.	D	23	
115.	C	55	
116.	D	19	
117.	A	20	
118.	D	20	
119.	C	21	
120.	D	20	
121.	C	55	
122.	C	172	
123.	D	305	Key word is "communication."
124.	D	8	
125.	A	123	
126.	A	169-170	
127.	D	39	
128.	B	38	
129.	A	82	

Professional Role

Question	Answer	Page
130.	B	75-76
131.	B	92
132.	B	209
133.	B	207
134.	D	74
135.	A	6
136.	C	25
137.	A	392-394, 431
138.	C	77
139.	B	28
140.	B	31

Systems/Legal and Regulatory

Question	Answer	Page
141.	D	212
142.	B	51
143.	B	79
144.	C	51
145.	D	51
146.	A	52
147.	C	59
148.	C	51
149.	B	62
150.	C	65-66
151.	B	63
152.	B	62
153.	D	62
154.	C	62
155.	A	53
156.	C	34
157.	C	81
158.	D	91
159.	A	67
160.	A	20

Education

Question	Answer	Page
161.	A	168
162.	B	167
163.	B	180
164.	B	168
165.	D	169
166.	C	174
167.	C	402
168.	A	167
169.	A	177
170.	C	179
171.	B	165
172.	A	289
173.	D	174
174.	D	315
175.	B	352-353
176.	C	169
177.	B	241-242
178.	B	231-232, 244
179.	D	394, 429-434
180.	B	125

Notes

Notes

Notes

Notes

Notes